A JOURNEY TO THE LIGHT WITHIN

Meditation for the Soul

Beth Lynch

BALBOA.
PRESS

A DIVISION OF HAY HOUSE

Balboa Press books may be ordered through booksellers or by contacting:

Balboa Press
A Division of Hay House
1663 Liberty Drive
Bloomington, IN 47403
www.balboapress.com
1 (877) 407-4847

Because of the dynamic nature of the Internet, any web addresses or links contained in this book may have changed since publication and may no longer be valid. The views expressed in this work are solely those of the author and do not necessarily reflect the views of the publisher, and the publisher hereby disclaims any responsibility for them.

The author of this book does not dispense medical advice or prescribe the use of any technique as a form of treatment for physical, emotional, or medical problems without the advice of a physician, either directly or indirectly. The intent of the author is only to offer information of a general nature to help you in your quest for emotional and spiritual well-being. In the event you use any of the information in this book for yourself, which is your constitutional right, the author and the publisher assume no responsibility for your actions.

Any people depicted in stock imagery provided by Getty Images are models, and such images are being used for illustrative purposes only.
Certain stock imagery © Getty Images.

ISBN: 978-1-9822-0938-4 (sc)
ISBN: 978-1-9822-0939-1 (e)

Print information available on the last page.

Balboa Press rev. date: 10/08/2018

CONTENTS

This book is dedicated to all of those who embark on the journey of understanding the depths of their Soul, embrace their Spirit and shine light to others, For it is in the light there will be peace on earth…

Beth Lynch

PRELUDE

I remember as a child asking God, "Why am I here"? Looking up into sky seemed like the "right" place to send the question. But I never "heard" anything come back. Now I can smile at my innocence and understand my fear in that. At the time I thought, "Why won't God answer me". Is it a stupid question?

The path of expectation, unworthiness and separation begins early!

The answers will always be right in front of us, revealing to us through our life experiences, relationships, choices and challenges. The challenge would be to recognize and allow it. Of course as a child, we are embracing the physical expression of the journey, because that is what we are taught. We are at the mercy of the perception of who is raising us and their foundation, if they even have one. We must keep in mind we have chosen our race, personality; qualities and weaknesses (challenges we learn most from).

There is one constant that I have come to know. That is the language of the Soul. This communication is often in metaphors and symbolic. It is constantly communicating through the energy fields of people, animals, air and all that is. It connects all matter and flows through us. We feel it through emotion and intuition. It carries a frequency which this creates the magnetic field around the physical body. It is this field in which we are in constant communication with people and all relationships. Imagine its force, connects, pulls and even repels all that is to us. Its language is for us to recognize and interpret and very importantly communicate with to our Self, Spirit and others.

This language will often be through emotions, subtle or strong. It will flow through our intuitive channels or sixth sense.

All senses are sensitive to this communication with the Soul, but because of the realm and subtle frequency the sixth is the most powerful. But do not exclude a vision, scent or voice. We must be open to all ways of this communication because we are Spirit and we are physical (matter).

In the A Journey to the Light Within there are a couple ways to use it. As a daily read for inspiration and meditation or as a six-week program of lessons, I also offer it as a correspondence course. Contact me if you are interested in taking me on the journeys with you! Either way, you will learn how to understand, receive and interpret the language of the Soul. This will be achieved by intention (personal commitment, meditation and the interpretation of personal experience). It will nurture your relationship with your intuitive voice, God or your higher power. It will open you to higher states of awareness in your personal relationships, choices and challenges and very importantly your Self.

Nikola Tesla's quote really says it all. "To understand the secrets of the Universe we must think in terms of energy, vibration and frequency". This is explaining the Law of Attraction, the magnetic force bringing to us, pushing or holding still all conditions based on our emotional frequencies we create by perception of life. The healing of the past, being active in our present will create our future. This is our Divine power and this is the Spiritual-Science of living.

As humans we have created a moral structure of sorts, where right or wrong (judgment), is always being pointed out and if we do not follow, bad things will happen. The concept of hell, a place we are sent if we do not follow rules or a certain book. Why would a loving God create such a place? Just another question with a lot of fear and the foundation to blame "someone," other than yourself. A concept I know I lived in fear with for the first two decades of my physical life. In the human concept of time it may not seem long but it felt longer.

Our relationship with God is taught, the approach very mental and technical. As we get older our search becomes more of a need and it is easy to get in our own way when our needs are not meant. That leaves a lot of responsibility on "God". So if we all take responsibility or respond to our abilities then we can join forces with the Divine Power within. There is no one or no one God to blame for where you feel you lack or need. You are responsible and when this accepted into the consciousness of one it helps many.

At some point our foundations become cracked and now "Why am I here" has a <u>need</u> to be answered with fear and sometimes desperation behind it. The crack is symbolic of our belief in any false security we may have created around ourselves. This will come in the form of relationships, finances, material belongings and false perceptions. Understand all things physical in your life is the creation of energy. Thought patterns plus emotional responses equal physical manifestation. In other words ask and you will receive.

The energy of emotion is the force behind all our thoughts and emotional responses. The mind is analyzing, dissecting as well as delivering these messages. If we have no discipline over our thought process and emotional responses then they run wild. This creates a magnetic force around us that is constantly pulling to or repelling people and experiences where we have the opportunity to learn and answer the questions that create the duality (Self and Spirit) are constantly trying to unite. Hence, war has begun.

I remember when our troops were called to duty in Iraq. I prayed and asked God, "Why are we still going to war, why haven't we learned from the past, it is not the way?" Two days later I was doing the dishes, gazing out the window at beautiful pine trees. I heard and felt these words flow through my mind. "As long as there is war in the Soul there will be war on earth". A chill went through me and a feeling of sadness. I understood the conflicts of the Soul and the battles our humanness struggles with. I thought to myself we have a long way to go as a species. Then a feeling or conscious knowing at that moment, not to <u>expect</u> everyone in my life personally and universally to be at the same place in their journey was ok. It seems to be almost impossible for us all to be enlightened at the same time and place and it was ok. Spiritual history has shown us that over and over.

But we do learn, heal and love in ways we did not know we were capable of when we unite our Souls journey with our physical expression. Compassion, forgiveness and love are the way to this. First for Self and you will then allow for others. The Journey Meditations will take you deep into the cracks to allow this relationship to be nurtured, understood and healed. Maybe it is one Soul at a time but one Soul touches many and carries that light into the energy of those relationships. Like an Olympic torch the light will touch many hearts.

Your questions will come to your conscious mind often in the journey, but so will the answers. You must be without expectation on the concept of time. As I shared, two days later doing the dishes is not where I "expected" to hear back. This is a feeling you cannot explain or even teach someone to have. It is within you to feel and it is trust, faith and love in the relationship with Self and Spirit that sets it free.

In the A Journey to the Light Within you will learn how to understand the communication between Spirit and Self. It is a feeling and will be understood as you journey deep into the light of your Spirit. Freeing the Self to express in the way it "needs" and DESERVES!

You have been drawn to the journey because of many reasons, curiosity, wanting a deeper meditation practice or desire to understand who you are. All of the reasons are important, personal and the calling of your Self and Spirit uniting as One. The Self (personality) and Spirit (Intuition, relationship with God) is treated as two separate entities. It must be acknowledged as One. Many express, I want to be more spiritual, but I have no time. When you understand each need each other to truly be in Divine expression you will realize time is not the problem, your commitment or lack or is. That can hurt to read and feel, but it is the truth you must accept or will very soon. That is if you choose to continue! I will be sharing with you actual experiences I have had in personal meditations as well as channeling for others. Often it will be in "their" words. Who are "they" I am often asked. Our loved ones crossed, Spiritual Masters, guides and yes, angels. It is Source, thee Source of Divine Intelligence, Love and Light we are all a part of and return to.

I will not direct energy trying to prove that to anyone. They are there, here, everywhere and we are worthy of the unconditional love and communication they offer. We are deserving to know we are not alone, ever no matter how old or young we are we deserve to claim the power within. Children are so close to this power. To see a room of twenty kids meditate and Om is one of the most humbling and powerful moments I have ever experienced. Many of them never having meditated before, they knew what to do more importantly they did not analyze or expect. Instead they allowed the connection of the Soul to be. They "felt" the naturalness.

How you go through your journey is your free will. One way is to use the A Journey to the Light Within "Meditations For the Soul" is on your own. Simply take yourself through the experience. Journaling is recommended, but not necessary. Another is to take me along for the journey. It will be a six week correspondence course via email will go through your daily practice and journal your experiences. Your journaling will be sent to me for interpretation. The interpretation will be done much like a reading. I will meditate and open to the highest wisdom and guidance for you. Your experiences beginning with your feelings will be what you are sending to me. You are guided how to begin with your journaling. It will take your meditations to a whole new level and open to you to your Soul's level of communication.

Every week there will be a theme for the meditations. I suggest you read the first day introduction of the each week completely so you have an understanding of how the meditations are done in conscious state. When you sit down for daily practice it is an option to create the atmosphere with a candle or incense. It is not necessary for meditation; the intention sets it in motion. It is about looking forward to this time of daily devotion, an act of self-love.

Your first read of the lesson is important; please do not skip this step. The intention will be set in motion and will become more natural and easier to achieve as you go along. Simple breathing techniques to prepare you for your meditation time are in every lesson. It is the signal to the nervous system that things are going to slow down, it is your first step to inner discipline! It has a profound effect on all that is you. It allows for all systems and cells to align with Divine frequency, allowing for a higher state of awareness and frequency in the body. When we resonate to higher frequency we are connection to the Divine Source, Intelligence and Light. We are connected to God, Higher Power, Buddha, Divine Mother and all who resonate in this Source. Spiritual Guides, Doctors and Angels, they are all amongst us. It is our Divine free will and right to be One with their presence, love and wisdom. When we meditate, pray, silence the mind and yes, connect with nature we align with this frequency. This is where Spiritual and physical healing will take place. The frequency of the physical is aligned and the body can and will heal. Understanding your energy system, symbols and metaphors is how communication with the Soul and Spirit is the most natural and empowering experience.

You will go through the journal and meditations immediately after. It is the journaling that you will send to me. You are guided on how to approach the journaling step by step. Whether you choose to take the journeys on your own or me with you, it will be personal, powerful and enlightening in every aspect of your life. You will be working. Your Self and Spirit will be uniting, and a deeper understanding of their needs revealed. This can be a sort of cleaning of the Spiritual closet. It can hurt a bit getting rid of what no longer fits or useful. Embrace the power of discernment.

I will return my interpretations to you, along with your next week's assignment. I will be approaching this just as I would a reading, with a blessing and complete surrender to the Divine and the wisdom and guidance being offered to you.

You will learn the symbolic language of the messages and how to recognize and trust your own intuitive knowings.

I have found that meditation is where the traditional and the metaphysical beliefs and perceptions become one. Through meditation, we can blur the boundaries between the two and venture into freedom of expression, healing, and creating. I look forward to holding your hand during the journey, and I further anticipate letting it go and watching you soar. My commitment to you is to be there to help guide you through the journey, as well as be an open channel for the guidance and energy that serves your highest good. In other words help you clean your closet.

Begin now, take a deep breath and repeat a few times this affirmation, then just three slow breaths and let it permeate around you. "I take responsibility for how I perceive life and respond to it. I am open to the Divine Communication that is here for me". I Am responding to my abilities as a Spiritual and a human being".

Be aware of how you "feel"..

We are thinking, feeling, intuitive and creative beings. We must embrace this perception and allow our natural and most Divine expression to be where we express from personally, professionally as a species. This is our Source to survival, it is natural, sacred and necessary for our survival.

Trust in the journey…
In Peace & Love. Beth Lynch

A JOURNEY TO THE LIGHT WITHIN

"Meditations For The Soul"

Welcome to A Journey to the Light Within, "Meditations For The Soul", a very personal journey of enlightenment and self discovery. The journey will be emotional and empowering. It will help you to know the Self and the Spirit as One. The conflict in one's journey is the separation that has occurred between the two. The war of the Self and Soul is also referenced as duality. It is in the understanding and healing of this duality we accept who we are and live a perception of life once believed only to be attained by the Masters, Spiritual hierarchy or in life after death.

Your self-discipline, Self awareness, and faith in your intuition will develop. You will learn the symbolic language of the Soul. It is metaphoric and symbolic. Often the challenge of a lifetime is to learn. You have embraced this language on some level or you would not be venturing deep into this journey. The wisdom and humble power you hold will be evident in all areas of your life. As well as concentration, willpower, and a loving relationship with your Self. This is extremely important, and sometimes misunderstood.

One must first recognize, accept and nurture the relationship with Self and Spirit in order to understand their relationship with the Divine Intelligence, Universe, and God. Call it what you like. As the Buddha shows it is enlightenment. What ever foundation you have created, followed or denounced we are all from One Source, an Intelligence of compassion and expression that we strive, search for and can attain.

In this understanding the personal relationships you have in the physical expression of your Spirit will flourish and you will be free to express your truth, creativity and light. Your journey will be nurturing for the mind, heart, body, and Soul. It will bring understanding to your past, clarity to your present and free you to create your future with more understanding, discipline and love The answer to why we are here is just beginning to unfold for you.

Remember: meditation requires practice. Be kind to your Self in coping with some of the distractions that may arise. Simple noises, inability to focus, and interruptions are to be expected. When we learn how to embrace distraction in meditation we learn how to handle what we perceive as distractions in our daily life.

One morning as I began to meditate I was thinking perfect, no one will interrupt me it was early and all was quiet. Well the roofers had an earlier than expected arrival. As I continued my breathing with a bit of tenseness running through I chose to be persistence and keep my focus on breath and the intention of the moment. Refusing to allow the less-than-positive emotions to take over, I continued breathing and just allowed the noises to exist around me. My meditation reflection (journaling) from that day became my most powerful entry for that week. In that moment, I learned so much about letting go and trusting in the process even when it seems you are distracted or interrupted the connection will still be happening. As we learn to embrace distractions in meditation, it will help us embrace them in our daily life. Instead of blaming or using them as an excuse for our happiness and even in the way of our Spiritual "time outs".

The journeys you are taking are action on the commitment to your meditation practice and nurturing your relationship with God. Literally the cells in your body will be lifting in frequency and healing on all levels will be in motion. An acceleration of Spiritual life force will flow through you. Self love and confidence are truly strengthened and in some a first.

Please be compassionate with yourself (patience runs out. compassion never does). If you begin to "feel" frustrated go back to your breathing. Take your time and have faith. It will become more natural as you go along. If you already have a practice you are comfortable with, you still will be creating a stronger connection to your Higher Self. Always be a humble student with no expectations, the Soul's journey is hard to put into words. It is a feeling, a knowing an experience one has to have to understand.

LESSON ONE

This lesson will help you to determine your direction and set your intentions for the next six weeks. It will become a strong foundation for you as your life continues in physical expression.

As the journey begins, you will learn how to take any distractions during your meditation time as well as in your daily life and put them in a Divine place. Your sacred box or shelf will become an important part of your week; you can now enjoy it and the power it has. Allow your path experience to be. Do not look for any one thing or outcome. This can be a challenge, but will become easier as the week goes on. It is one of your simplest yet powerful Spiritual tools for you to use not only in meditation but in daily life experiences.

Undertaking the journey with no expectations will open you to more than you could imagine. And when this attitude is "practiced" in meditation, it will flow naturally into a way of life. This mindset, coupled with the idea of embracing distraction during meditation, helps one to embrace the distractions of life. These concepts will be practiced throughout the next six weeks in hopes of transitioning them into a natural way of being that you'll take with you after this program is complete. If we are working, contact me if these concepts are still difficult after the second day.

In this first lesson of the journey, you will learn how to trust your own knowings, intuition and feelings. In order to do this, you must connect with and trust the light within. This light is symbolic of your Spirit, Oneness with all, God, Universe, and Buddha. Buddha is enlightened One, you have chosen to enlighten by your intention and commitment to this journey.

The breath is the way into the light. It tells the mind to still, emotions to calm and body to relax. It sends the signal to just be, freeing the light to shine through you. Recognize It, embrace It and commit to It. I have capitalized the reference to breath as "It" to show respect the gift of breath and the power it connects you to when you direct and consciously breathe. It opens you to the light, it moves through lower emotions, calms anxiety and clears the intuitive channels that are connected to the higher frequencies where Divine communication takes place.

We will focus on breath awareness and growing comfortable in our Sacred Space. In order to achieve this, we must learn how to be alone with our Self. Our Self holds the energy of who we are, which is reflected in our personality our responses to situations, choices, and challenges in our everyday life. Everyday life: what a great place to begin!

You have already made the commitment to your personal growth and power, spiritually, mentally, emotionally and physically — by committing to the A Journey to the Light Within. Congratulations on the self-discipline and the desire you are already expressing!

Often, there is a resistance to being alone or still in thought. In meditation you will learn how to look forward to this time, to discover feelings of lightness, strength, and peace within it. Let us not forget that time spent alone is a loving gesture toward the Self.

You will first create a Sacred Space in which to meditate in every day or night. Comfort is important, but remembers this is about conscious meditation so do not make it easy on yourself to fall asleep. It is important to journal immediately after meditation, as subconscious experiences will often flow as you are writing. Even if you feel you did not experience anything or were unable to stay focused, you will still be feeling something. It is this that will help you get to know you on another level. If we are working together, I will help you with this as we get closer to meditation time. If you are going through on your own, it will be a great way to look back on what you have experienced and how far you really have come.

What is meditation? There are many definitions, but first remember this: it is a combination of intention, which you have now put in motion, breath awareness, which you are learning and allowing yourself to trust the experiences as they occur. The latter may be your biggest challenge — but I'm happy to help you! Being conscious in meditation means you will be aware of the noises around you, along with subconscious thoughts and emotions that enter into your awareness. That is why you will create that sacred shelf, box or file. You will direct them into the file or box or set them on the shelf. In all its simplicity, it is stopping the energy or emotional attachment to interfere with the meditation.

If you are feeling too tired to meditate or in need of energy, you will come out of meditation energized and alert. Often a five-minute meditation can be a great way to energize. You may be asking, How does that work? Understanding from the technical standpoint it comes down to the vibration or frequency of the body, which is determined by our thought patterns and emotional responses. Often in daily life we can lower our vibration because of our perceptions, emotions and thoughts. This also will weaken the immune system. In meditation or prayer, we naturally bring the body to a higher frequency. In higher states of awareness we allow the mind, body and Spirit to unite, bringing frequency to its most natural and powerful healing rhythm. It is this natural energy that gives the body what it needs to re-energize and resist all discord and dis-ease. So, why not do this for your Self every day?

Meditation is always an opportunity for wisdom and guidance, though they're not always achieved during the "physical time" of meditation. Instead, trust that in meditation, you are opening your intuitive pathways for your messages and knowings. It is important not to feel let down if you do not "get" anything immediately as a result of your meditation. You have opened the energy with intention to receive. It has been done. Once you start doubting meditation, you are questioning your ability to be connected to your light and encouraging self judgment. An emotional attachment will be made to this failure creating disappointment and even frustration. This does not make it wrong, it may happen and you will learn from it if it does.

Keep in mind; you may have to refer back to your meditation assignment in order to complete it. I suggest you read <u>Day One</u> once completely and then begin. You will become familiar with how the meditation will go. Remember it is fine to go back to it if you forget a step especially as the meditations get longer. You are stretching your ability to meditate consciously.

Lesson One Meditation Assignment

Please read at least once before beginning! Avoid times of day that are difficult for you to be alert. Do not rush; time should not be issue. Remember, time is not measured in Spirit as we know it. It is a human concept that we will move away from. In Spirit it is referenced as sequence. This will be a powerful part of your experience as you begin to naturally embrace this concept. Much of the stress you experience has a "time" measurement creating more "pressure" than if you embraced the synchronicity (natural flow of situation, instead of outcome or "when").

Have a notebook, journal, or computer (recommended, if we are working together) ready so you can journal immediately after meditation. Keep in mind to ask questions, if you have an experience you do not understand while in meditation. For example, if you sense a presence, ask, Who are you? Or if you recognize them, embrace them with a hello.

Other possible questions include, what does this mean for me? Keep open to the simplicity of the presence of Spirit Guides, loved ones crossed, etc. They are always with us and, in these quiet and sacred times, can be seen, felt or sensed.

After your meditation, the first line of your entry will be: At this time I feel... Then, write any emotion you're feeling at that moment: sadness, happiness, anxiety, peace, etc. Continue writing any thoughts, feelings, knowings, etc. that come to the conscious mind. Do not try to remember. We are practicing releasing the mental and from self-judgment.

If you do not remember anything, go back to step one. Write what you are feeling and go from there. There are no wrong experiences! You will learn how to let go of any judgment you may inflict on your Self that is being destructive to you. Exceptions do not serve any meditation.

Prepare for Meditation

Create a comfortable environment. If you are tired, please sit up with your spine straight to keep yourself from falling asleep.

Create in your mind a sacred shelf or box where you will place all distractions. If your distraction is a person in your life, then you will simply say or think, I place you on the shelf at this time to be blessed and in Divine Order. You may have to do this many times, or not at all. What is important is that you are letting go of any less-than-positive emotions and/or distractions that would have connected to you. These emotions are in your energy or they would not be revealed. You are disciplining your emotional response. You are being active as opposed to reactive!

Remember all the sacred tools you use in the program can be used throughout the week, course, and life! Below begin to read and follow along, you will know when to close your eyes.

- Begin with breath awareness.
- Inhale slowly and comfortably.
- Count silently to 4 as you breathe in.
- Exhale to 6 slowly, comfortably.
- Imagine filling your lower belly with air like a balloon.
- Let the air release naturally, then gently contract the belly to push out air from the lungs.
- Remember to be as natural as possible. The rhythm will begin to take over after a few moments. TRUST.
- Repeat for 8 breaths. Now close your eyes and open after the next step to continue. Smile…
- Now increase your inhale breath to 6 and your exhale breath to 8.
- Allow for 8 breaths, allow your breathing to flow into a natural rhythm.

Tell yourself, silently or aloud, to relax around the eyes. Allow this feeling to drift down to your shoulders, your arms, your hands, your palms, and your fingers.

Shift your awareness to your heart. Allow the intention to relax, to flow gently down through your torso, feet, toes. Breathe… Take three breaths. Smile…

Now, bring awareness to your heart light by imagining (see, feel, or know) that a gold flame is in your heart. Trust. Breathe the light gently, with intention and imagination, up to the center of your forehead. <u>Your eyes can be open or closed.</u>

This is your Third Eye, or as I will refer to it as the Divine Eye.

Hold the light for 4 breaths behind eyes, forehead and let it flow back like it is filling a tunnel with light. Imagination! <u>Close your eyes as you hold the light in Divine Eye.</u>

Return to the heart and lift the light once again to the Divine Eye and hold. This time, allow for 8 breaths. <u>Close eyes again.</u>

Continue illuminating a tunnel with light. This encourages the area behind the eyes to relax. As well as stimulates the energy opening you to intuitive guidance.

See, feel or just know that you are standing, facing a path behind your eyes. Give yourself permission to walk the path.

Repeat: "At this time, I embrace my Divine path". Just allow yourself to "be" for a few moments. Breathe, and just embrace the experience. Smile…

When you feel it is time to return, bring awareness back into your breath.

This may occur as a subtle knowing, or maybe a feeling of "waking up." When it does, just begin breath awareness.

Breathe with awareness into the sound of the breath and the flow of the body. Open your eyes slowly, and allow your senses to adjust. Take 3 strong breaths.

Journal

- Begin with; My feelings (emotions) at this time are… Follow that with whatever comes to your conscious mind.

Repeat this meditation daily. Each day give your self permission to go further down the path. Embrace the feelings, knowing, colors or sounds that you have.

If you feel the presence, whether someone you know has crossed over or a spiritual figure (traditional or personal) simply acknowledge them with a smile. If you like, pose a question or thought without expectation of an immediate answer. Allow yourself to go down the path further each day. Trust you imagination. If it is an image, it is real.

Conclusion

This week is about exercising the Third Eye or we will refer to it as the Divine Eye. This is the Eye that sees from the highest perception. It will always reveal the sacred truth of your experiences.

It will reveal to you what is above the human desire and need and let you see what is for your highest good. Remember it may be a symbol or metaphor as well as literal. Try not to ANALYZE. Write it down immediately so you do not influence with subconscious fear or need. Do not judge or focus on what does not appear logical. It is the language of the Soul and you are learning how to understand and communicate. Trust it will come together.

LESSON TWO

In this meditation lesson we will be learning how to separate the lower vibrational emotions and thought patterns (conscious and subconscious).

Think of it as moving through the dark spaces or shadows of our with our Self and others.

We will begin with the relationship we have with our Self. The term Self is the personality, the part of you that is connected to the emotional and mental atmospheres closest to the physical you are expressing.

The relationship is the energy created by how you respond emotionally, thoughts and actions. Anyone connected to relationship is also contributing. You are creating the condition of the relationship and therefore responsible for it. Everything you have an energy exchange with is a relationship, people, careers, finances, health and God.

All relationships are opportunities to learn about your Self. In the physical expression of our relationships we tend to attach. We are here to learn not to do just that. We become very re-active emotionally when our sense of security is threatened. Often this comes from fearing of losing what we have become attached to. Fear becomes the foundation and eventually the relationship will crack or break.

In the language of the Soul metaphors and symbols are often used to show the relationship from a higher perception. This will separate you from the details you have already gone over and over in your mind. If there are lower vibrations transmitting to one another, then they are transmitting through your body as well. Waiting to create stress, dis-comfort or even dis-ease. It is in this lesson you will learn how to recognize and release these energies.

The metaphors and symbols will step you out of the details and allow you to separate from the details you have and allow you to see the bigger picture. This frees you to the strength and clarity and truth of the relationship and puts you in a place of power to create the future.

In our relationships we are often emotionally re-active. You will now become active. You will begin letting go of the baggage you have been carrying and travel through your experiences lighter with an open heart, mind and Spirit. This openness will free you to the communication with your Self, Spirit and others.

We will begin with the dark spaces, because they are symbolic of the emotional baggage we have stored away connected to the interaction we have in relationships, past and present. The anger, sadness, pain, the energy of unforgiveness and all lower frequency patterns of thought. A reminder this energy is creating the present condition of your present relationships and the future of them.

Let's refrain from the labels negative/positive or bad/good because it creates a subconscious foundation that you will create from. It also energizes self judgment and criticism toward the Self which will then be placed on others. These emotions create repetitive experiences and havoc in the emotional and physical body. Such as low self esteem, depression, anxiety, dis-comfort and dis-ease. It is also connected to the ways in which we have in the past and may in the present be responding <u>to the conditions in our life.</u> (By conditions, what has come to be in our relationships with self, others, finances, health and all physical expression.) It is also how we have processed painful events in our life. We will begin with understanding experiences, that we have processed negative or bad as lower frequency and positive or good experiences as higher frequency. In this perception you will begin to immediately separate your energy from these experiences which in turn begins or accelerates the higher understanding (perception shift) and the healing will take its course.

Relationship interactions are where we will learn the most about ourselves. As we interact, we must be open to learn about ourselves in the relationship. This is where you begin, the perception! In every relationship, we must be able to communicate and to express who we are emotionally, mentally, physically, and spiritually. We must be able to express our feelings and creative energies. If not, we will be in conflict with our truth and not be fulfilled. This will create a weak foundation in the relationship. Which can create insecurity, fear, resentment, anger, or any other lower vibrational frequency. We will then hold these frequencies in our bodies. They will travel through us via the chakras, the nervous system and endocrine system will deliver into our physical systems. Stress, vulnerable immune system, discord or dis-ease is how the body will express this energy.

Keep your relationship priority in order, it is important. I found it interesting to write which should come first, God or Self, Self or God. One will strongly influence the other or take the other by the hand. So I decided to say it both ways.

First, let's take care of Self. When taking care of your Self first your relationship with God or your higher belief, or Spirit will create a magnetic

field of Divine energy through and around you. You will then be creating your life from this frequency. Creating a clearer perception of what is for your highest good and not what your desire body is needing or trying to satisfy itself with. To place this pressure upon another person, material things, financial security or any experience will set you up for disappointment. It may take "time" but the consequences will reveal in your emotional and mental peace of mind, joy and perception.

When we take care of our relationship to God first well what it feels like to think is like a shortcut to peace of mind, joy and a beautiful perception of life. It is not easy to explain or put into words. Many of you reading this know what it means, others you are on your way to know.

Every relationship we are in, is an opportunity to learn about our Self. The closer we are to someone, the more sensitive to the expression we will be. In order to do this with another person, we must first understand the relationship with the Self and Spirit — the Self being the personality, qualities, beliefs, and challenges, and the Spirit being communication with God. God represents the belief in a Higher Intelligence — belief in a light shines in all darkness, belief in the fact that there is something to learn from and ascend from in all life's experiences. This can be expressed in many ways from the traditional to the metaphysical.

In turn, we stop the search from outside ourselves to "make" us happy. You will no longer place pressure on to another person or material things to "make" us happy. True fulfillment comes from within. There is a sense of peace and security within that is felt and no one can take it. Because no "one" gave it to us. We embraced the language of the Soul and communication with God is free to be. It is our Divine Inheritance, we not only deserve, but require. It is what one must discover and utilize to be in the true expression of life.

This week we will bring light into the darkness of our relationships when we heighten our awareness about them. We create the conditions; they are not created for us. By living in this truth, you empower your Self and Spirit to work together.

In your "Let Go, Let In" journal you will reveal your thought patterns and emotions clearly to your Self. In this instance, you are declaring your power to direct and discipline your thoughts and the energy connected to them.

There is often a resistance to going deeper into a relationship, because it gives us the responsibility clean up the "condition" of it. Let's compare it to cleaning one room at a time as opposed to cleaning the whole house!

Healing the relationship with our Self is always a priority, but it is through our energy exchange with others that we will learn the most about our Self. To take the time to know and feel our thoughts and emotions by separating from them, we create the time and place to clear our intuitive channels. The questions, Should I be in this relationship?, Will we be together?, or What did I do wrong?, will no longer be answered by anyone else than yourself. Imagine knowing the answers. It is empowering and humbling.

To release the Self from self-judgment, anger, fear, and repetitive thoughts that pull down a relationship frees the experience to be in Divine Truth and Light. Meaning you are able to express your love, creative gifts, create abundance and live the life you deserve. You will also know instinctively when a relationship, job or situation has taken its course. When you have learned all you can from the relationship and respect your (and your partners) desire to move on. To inhibit a relationship from expressing itself in the highest way will limit the individual's ability to love, heal, and grow within it. This creates, for many, unhappy endings or states of confusion in a relationship. The "title" of the relationship can be in all ways, personal, professional and financial. It can and will influence your happiness and how you perceive life.

Also, remember that the body will take on the lower frequency, which in turn creates stress, weakens the immune system and affect ones health. Other factors on the body's response are family, environment and Spiritual foundation.

Keep this formula in mind; it is universal law: <u>Thought plus emotional response equals future manifestation.</u> In other words, every thought you have will carry a vibration. Your emotional response to the thought will create the frequency flowing through you via the endocrine and nervous systems, a frequency which then finds its place in the body. As you do the following exercise you will be separating these energies. It is then the less positive frequency will rise to higher frequency. Becoming active and not reactive, empowered not powerless, disciplining and not out of control.

In the "Let Go, Let In" journaling, you'll separate positive thought and emotion from less than positive. Then you will be able to set clear intention and recognize what is for the highest good of the relationship. You will also free your Self to accept all truth for relationship. From there, you'll create the dynamics of the relationship and allow it to express to its Divine ability. Whether the relationship is meant to be in physical expression forever or an experience you carry in your heart, mind, and soul, you create the future of it and all other relationship from this perception. It will be a strong foundation for you to exist in and create relationships from. You will express your truth, creativity and light. Living in joy, learning and healing with Self and others is a Divine right we all have.

Lesson Two Meditation Assignment

Please read through meditation once before beginning.

You will want to have two notebooks or journals; write "Let Go" on the cover of one, and "Let In" on the other. Begin with choosing a relationship, past or present that creates lower vibrational emotions when you think about it. Remember we are going to use the Soul language from now on to separate from the details of the relationship. This will be symbolic and in metaphors.

In the "Let Go" journal, you will be releasing energy in this specific relationship that causes you confusion, sadness, fear, anger, anxiety, etc. Or, in other words, you'll be releasing what you need to let go of in order to be in a place of peace.

On the first page of your "Let Go" journal, write: "I release all thought patterns and emotional responses that no longer serve my Divine Truth of my journey".

The "Let In" journal records anything you are grateful for, have learned, and love about the relationship. On the first page of your "Let In" journal write this affirmation: I embrace the Divine Truth and acceptance of my journey today.

Always begin with "Let Go" journal first and make a list of what you would like to let go of from the relationship; please send this with your next journal assignment. Be sure to choose a significant relationship, present or past, which you have experienced.

Next, make a list of anything that you are grateful for in that relationship. Keep your focus on the relationship, not the person. This can be a challenge, because we tend fixate on what the person does or does not do. You only need to do this once. The rest of your journaling will be for each day, but if something comes up connected to the relationship please put it in the journal.

- You will now take a few deep breaths and close your eyes.
- Bring to your awareness a relationship you are in, present or past.

- Focus on one in which some negative emotions (anger, fear, sadness, confusion) or uncomfortable memories still exist. This relationship could be with someone you do not understand or even get along with. <u>Past or present.</u>

We are going to take a look at the "condition" of this relationship with a spouse, significant other, parent, son or daughter, sibling, or friend. Remember: there is no time in energy. (All emotional responses and thought patterns about the relationship have created this energy and the way the relationship plays out.) Therefore, this relationship can be from the past as well as from the present. The power of this is, it will create the future of the relationship and other relationships you are in. Remember, the universal law is always in motion. We will attract like a magnet who we are and we are what we think and feel about ourselves and others.

We will work with the relationship energy you have chosen first, and then transition to a daily journal. Complete the relationship journaling first. You only have to complete the relationship "Let Go" and "Let In" journaling once this week. The other days will be your daily "Let Go" and "Let In." If the relationship comes up for that day, please include it, but it's not necessary to focus only on the relationship each day. Your journaling should preferably be done before bedtime.

Again, your journaling does not have to be specifically about that relationship, unless it comes up to you, but do always try to bring in something not connected to the relationship as well. The exercises below will help you get started.

<u>"Let Go" Journal</u> – Any emotions or emotional responses you have experienced during the day that you wish to shift or no longer experience.

<u>"Let In" Journal</u> – Any emotion you are grateful for or are happy to feel. Continue your "Let Go, Let In" journal daily, along with the following meditation. Keep in mind that this does not have to be about the relationship.

Any thoughts or emotions are welcomed. Journal the "Let Go, Let In" before you meditate and following meditation.

Day One

- Begin with your Inner Light Meditation you practiced in week one.
- Create a bench up on the path.
- Allow your Self to approach the bench and sit.
- As you sit on the bench, you will move into breath awareness and a mantra.
- Inhale "DIVINE" exhale "ACCEPTANCE". Continue for a minimum of 7 breaths.
- Sit on bench without expectations. Just "be." Breathe…
- Allow your Self to be on the bench by your Self. Embrace the view in you have as you sit on the bench. Just breathe your mantra. Let the peace and healing enter your being. It is happening for you.
- Be aware of how you feel.
- When it is time to get up from bench you will know. Trust this.
- Say aloud or silently before you leave the bench, "I embrace the Divine Truth and acceptance in all my relationships. I share this with all facets of my Self and all relationships, past, present and future". Breathe…just be.

Each day could be different. Embrace this fact, and release yourself from the concept of time or expectation from any relationship. See, know, or simply allow yourself to get up from bench and return down the path, back to awareness and where journey began. Take at least 3 strong breaths; allow your senses to adjust. Remember smile.

Journal

Remember begin with how your feeling. Write, I feel at this time ……… and just continue flowing in feelings and thoughts. Trust your Self and Spirit are communicating.

Day Two

- Today you will be inviting the person in the relationship from the Let Go journal to sit on bench with you. Take a moment now for this intention to be sent out.

Please do not expect them to appear. You may see, feel or know their presence. What is most important is the energy connection is made.

- Begin with your Inner Light Meditation.
- Create a bench up on the path.
- Allow your Self to approach the bench and sit.
- As you sit on the bench, you will move into breath awareness and a mantra.
- Inhale "DIVINE" exhale "TRUTH." Continue for a minimum of 7 breaths.
- Exist without expectations. Just "be." Breathe…
- Be aware of how you feel.
- <u>Now, invite the person in the relationship</u> discussed above to sit on the bench. Simply think or say, I invite you, for the higher good of our relationship, to sit with me on this bench. When it is time to get up from bench you will know. Trust this.
- Each day could be different. Embrace this fact, and release yourself from the concept of time. See, know, or simply allow yourself to get up from bench and return down the path, back to awareness and where journey began.
- Say aloud or silently, I embrace the light and send it to all facets of myself and relationships I am in, past, present and future Breathe… Allow… Be…
- You have acknowledged your dark spaces and are now sending them light.

<u>Journal</u>

Days Three and Four

- Begin your meditation as before.
- On these days you will <u>invite the person in the relationship</u> discussed above to sit on the bench.
- Go to your bench up on the path. Allow yourself to approach the bench and sit. As you sit on the bench, you will move into breath awareness and a mantra.
- Inhale "DIVINE; exhale "ACCEPTANCE" Continue for a minimum of 7 breaths…
- It is time to invite the person in the relationship discussed above to sit on the bench. Simply think or say, I invite you, for the higher good of our relationship, to sit with me on this bench.
- Just allow… Begin with a smile…
- Be aware of how you "feel."
- Engage in conversation if you "feel," and say anything that comes to mind, anything you wish you could say or wish you did say. This is a sacred time for you and that person for the highest good.
- Tell him or her, Thank you for being here.
- Allow for a sense of peace and just "be."
- Leave your bench the same way each time, or embrace another way if it is revealed to you.

Journal

Begin with how you feel.

Day Five

This time invite anyone to the bench you'd like, the same one, another person, anyone you wish.

- It can be someone you are happy with or someone you feel you would like to communicate better with.
- Or just sit on the bench and see who shows up!
- Every time you visit the bench, allow your Self to just be. No expectations.
- Embrace emotions, symbols, colors, etc. Ask questions if you have them!

Journal

Conclusion

This lesson was about going into the different emotions of relationships... You may have surprised yourself who may have come to your bench. Trust what served your highest good were there. Use this exercise anytime you would like to understand a relationship more or if you have a conflict in one. Remember past or present, energy cords can and will be connected whether someone is in your life or not. Even if someone has crossed over to the Spirit world, the energy between will still be connected.

When you separate these emotions it allows you to see the highest truth of the relationship. It offers you understanding and the freedom to heal. You are free to learn about your Self and the Spirit is free to express through you. You will then draw to you relationships that all you are able to express your love and creative energies.

LESSON THREE

In this lesson, we will be tuning into the vibration and frequency of our energy system. This will be done by connecting to the sound of each chakra. To understand our energy system, we must first understand the chakras. How they resonate and the energies connected to them.

Imagine the chakras as energy doorways in the astral body. The astral body surrounds the physical body and is invisible to the physical eye. It is, however, seen through intuitive knowing and the Third Eye, or the sixth sense. It can be measured by its frequency, color, and sound. There are various approaches to understanding this system. We all have a bit of natural instinct, which we have either nurtured or suppressed along the way. Traditional family (tribal) beliefs, fears, and environment can also influence this foundation. We have evolved as a consciousness to where this ancient wisdom serves us to understand and incorporate it into our daily life. Our health, wealth and happiness will benefit tremendously from an understanding of the energy system.

There is a magnetic field or an aura that surrounds the physical body (and all living things). The chakras are the portals that the energy frequency created by your thought patterns and emotions will travel through. It is this magnetic force that attracts experiences from which you will learn from to you. This will be experienced in all relationships. All experiences are relationships. For example, you have a relationship with your Self, God, other people, finances, and career. The perception you hold about these will affect the condition of these relationships. Even though they are separate there is a domino effect that is always connecting them.

Everything is a relationship, and with this knowledge, you will begin to understand your choices and challenges from past and present. It will free you to create healthy and abundant relationships in your future! By taking this course, you have chosen to nurture your relationship with your Self and with your Spirit. These are the most important relationships you'll have.

Every thought and emotional response carries with it a vibration, which in turn travels through you. The vibration's intensity will be measured by how much emotion is connected to it and how often you think it. Next, you must observe if your patterns are positive or less-than-positive. I prefer to let go of the words "negative" or "bad," because they instill judgment toward the Self or others. One of our greatest lessons is to free ourselves from judgment.

Each chakra is connected to the physical body and its systems — the organs and muscles, plus the circulatory, nervous, and endocrine systems. Every system and cell will be affected by this invisible system, and the charkas influence health tremendously. Beginning with the personal commitment you've made to understand and discipline your thoughts and emotional responses to situations, you are healing and empowering all relationships — past, present, and future!

Each chakra corresponds to a color and a vibration. Red, the root chakra, can compare to the beat of a drum; the crown, white and/or gold, carries with it the sound of an angelic melody. Understanding frequency and how it affects the body will heighten your awareness of the sense of sound and feeling and your body's response to it.

The understanding of the energy system, and the realization that we are and everything we think, feel, and act on is energy is empowering. This understanding allows us to utilize the system to heal and to create the life we deserve.

The transformation of lower vibrational thought and emotion to higher thoughts and emotions, or the transformation of less-than-positives into positives. Where else, but in our relationship with the Self, personal relations and careers, or fulfilling acts will we be able to express this?

Lesson Three Meditation

PLEASE READ DAY ONE COMPLETELY SO YOU UNDERSTAND
BEFORE YOU BEGIN THE STEPS. IT WILL MAKE IT EASIER
FOR YOU FOR AS YOU GO THROUGH THE LESSON.

We will be tuning into these frequencies with the power of chanting, calling on the seven sacred sounds that connect to your chakras. You will also be using your imagination and visualization. Each chakra will begin as a rosebud. As you inhale, you will remain silent and let it be as comfortable and as natural as possible. It will become more natural every day.

Day One: Visualization and Sound Meditation

<u>Begin at base of spine / Root Chakra</u>

Sitting is preferred for this meditation, make yourself comfortable.

- Begin your breath awareness. Take seven breaths; inhale to 4, and exhale to 6.
- Bring your awareness to the base of your spine. Imagine a red rose facing down toward Mother Earth.
- Inhale slowly and naturally.
- Allow the petals of the red to be your focus.
- As you inhale, gently focus on the rose's red petals.
- As you exhale, let the petals begin to open as you create the sound "Lam." (The "a" will be pronounced as "aaaahhhh.") Allow the rose to open as you exhale.
- Repeat seven times. See the petals open, and focus on the ruby-red glow emanating from the rose. Allow the glow to flow through you and around you.
- Maintain a natural and comfortable flow throughout, resting in the color.
- Allow your next three breaths to be free from thought. Just breathe…
- With your next inhalation, bring your awareness to your lower belly, behind the navel. Imagine an orange rosebud, facing out.
- Inhale slowly and naturally.
- Allow the petals of the orange rosebud to be your focus.
- As you inhale, gently focus on the orange petals.
- As you exhale, allow the petals to begin to open as you create the sound "Vam." (The "a" will be pronounced as "aaaahhhh.") Allow the rose to open as you exhale.
- Repeat seven times. Keep a natural and comfortable flow throughout, resting in the color.
- Allow your next three breaths to be free from thought. Just breathe…
- Next, inhale. Bring awareness to the center of your torso. Imagine a yellow rosebud, facing out.
- Inhale slowly and naturally.
- Allow the petals of the yellow rosebud to be your focus.
- As you inhale, gently focus on the yellow petals.

A Journey to the Light Within

- As you exhale, allow the petals to begin to open as you create the sound "Ram." (The "a" will be pronounced as "aaaahhhh.") Allow the rose to open as you exhale.

- Repeat seven times. Keep a natural and comfortable flow throughout, resting in the color.

- Allow your next three breaths to be free from thought. Just breathe…

- Allow yourself to just "be" in the yellow. Repeat silently as you inhale "Divine" and exhale "Power." Just "be" for a few moments. Enjoy the divine power flowing through your consciousness.

- After a few moments, or when you "feel" you are aware of present surroundings, breathe the yellow light into every pore of your being. Let it come to be a flame in your heart, and just be aware of how you feel.

Journal—At this time "I feel…".

Begin your journaling now, remembering to free yourself from expectations. Just be aware of how you feel, and record anything that comes to your conscious mind.

Day Two: Visualization and Sound Meditation

<u>Begin at Center Torso / Solar Plexus</u>

This is your solar plexus, or third chakra. The symbolic yellow rosebud will be our tool to access the energy of the chakra.

- Preferably sitting, make yourself comfortable.
- Begin your breath awareness.
- Take 7 breaths, inhaling to 4, exhaling to 6.
- Direct your awareness to your center torso.
- Imagine a yellow rosebud facing out. Remember: see, feel, or just know! Not everyone sees, so just trust it is happening. This can be a challenge, so go with it.
- Inhale slowly and naturally.
- Allow the petals of the yellow rose to be your focus.
- As you inhale, gently focus on the rose's yellow petals.
- As you exhale, allow the petals to begin to open as you create the sound "Ram." (The "a" will be pronounced as "aaaahhhh.") Allow the rose to open as you exhale.
- Repeat seven times. See the petals open and focus on the yellow glow coming from the rosebud. Allow the glow to flow through you and around you.
- Maintain a natural and comfortable flow throughout, resting in the color.
- Allow your next three breaths to be free from thought. Just breathe…
- With your next inhalation, bring your awareness to your center chest, the heart chakra. Imagine an emerald green rosebud, facing out.
- Inhale slowly and naturally.
- Allow the emerald green rose petals to be your focus.
- As you inhale, gently focus on the green petals.
- As you exhale, allow the petals to begin to open as you create the sound "Yam." (The "a" will be pronounced as "aaahhh.") Allow the rose to open as you exhale.
- Repeat seven times. Maintain a natural and comfortable flow throughout, resting in the color.
- Allow your next three breaths to be free from thought. Just breathe…
- With your next inhalation, bring your awareness to your throat. Imagine a sapphire blue rosebud, facing out.

- Inhale slowly and naturally.
- Allow the sapphire blue petals to be your focus.
- As you inhale, gently focus on the blue petals.
- As you exhale, allow the petals to begin to open as you create the sound "Ham." (The "a" will be pronounced as "aaaahhhh.") Allow the rose to open as you exhale…
- Repeat seven times. Keep a natural and comfortable flow throughout, resting in the color.
- Allow your next three breaths to be free from thought. Just breathe….
- Allow yourself to just "be" in the beautiful blue light. Repeat silently as you inhale "Divine" and exhale "Love." Just "be" for a few moments. Enjoy the divine power flowing through your being.
- After a few moments, or when you "feel" you are aware of your present surroundings, breathe the light into every pore of your being. Let it come to be a flame in your heart, and just be aware of how you feel.

Journal

Begin your journaling now, remembering to free yourself from expectations. Just be aware of how you feel, and record anything that comes to your conscious mind.

Day Three:

Begin with the Heart Chakra

- Sitting, make yourself comfortable. Awareness at the center of chest.

- Begin your breath awareness. Take seven breaths, inhaling to four, exhaling to six.

- Inhale slowly and naturally.

- Inhale, bringing your awareness to your center chest, the heart chakra. Image an emerald green rosebud, facing out.

- Inhale slowly and naturally.

- Allow the emerald green petals to be your focus.

- As you inhale, gently focus on the green petals.

- As you exhale, allow the petals to begin to open as you create the sound "Yam." (The "a" will be pronounced as "aaahhhh.") Allow the rose to open as you exhale…

- Repeat seven times. Keep a natural and comfortable flow throughout, resting in the color.

- Allow your next three breaths to be free from thought. Just breathe…

- With your next inhalation, bring awareness to your throat. Imagine a sapphire blue rosebud, facing out.

- Inhale slowly and naturally.

- Allow the sapphire blue petals to be your focus.

- As you inhale, gently focus on the blue petals.

- As you exhale, allow the petals to begin to open as you create the sound "Ham." (The "a" will be pronounced as "aaahhhh.") Allow the rose to open as you exhale…

- Repeat seven times. Keep a natural and comfortable flow throughout, resting in the color.

- Allow your next three breaths to be free from thought. Just breathe…

- With your next inhalation, bring awareness to your center forehead. This is the Third Eye or Divine Eye. Imagine a purple rosebud, facing out.

- Inhale slowly and naturally.

- Allow the purple petals to be your focus.

- As you inhale, gently focus on the purple petals.

- As you exhale, allow the petals to begin to open as you create the sound "Om." (Inhale silence; exhale "aaahhhh… oooo… mmmm." Relax on the inhale in order to allow for natural flow.
- Repeat seven times. Maintain a natural and comfortable flow throughout, resting in the color.
- Allow your next three breaths to be free from thought. Just breathe…
- Repeat seven times. Maintain a natural and comfortable flow throughout, resting in the purple light.
- Allow yourself to just "be" in the beautiful purple light.
- Repeat silently as you inhale "Divine" and exhale "Truth."
- Just "be" for a few moments. Enjoy the Divine Light flowing through your being.
- After a few moments, or when you "feel" you are aware of your present surroundings, breathe the white light into every pore of your being.
- Allow it to grow into a flame in your heart, and just be aware of how you feel.

Journal

Begin your journaling now, remembering to free yourself from expectations. Just be aware of how you feel, and record anything that comes to your conscious mind.

Day Four

<u>Begin at the Forehead The Divine Eye</u>

- Sitting, make yourself comfortable.
- Begin your breath awareness. Take seven breaths, inhaling to four, exhaling to six.
- Inhale slowly and naturally.
- Imagine a purple rosebud, facing out.
- Inhale slowly and naturally.
- Allow the petals of the purple rosebud to be your focus.
- As you inhale gently, focus on the purple petals.
- As you exhale, allow the petals to being to open as you create the sound "Om."
- (Inhale silence; exhale "Aaaa…oooo…mmmm.")
- <u>Relax on the inhale</u> in order to allow for natural flow as you <u>create sound on exhale.</u>
- Repeat seven times. Keep a natural and comfortable flow throughout, resting in the color.
- Allow your next three breaths to be free from thought. Just breathe…
- With your next inhalation, bring your awareness to just above the crown. Imagine a white rosebud facing up.
- Inhale slowly and naturally.
- Allow the petals of the white rose to be your focus.
- As you inhale, gently focus on the white petals. Allow them to open as you exhale.
- Let go of all thought, feel white, and just "be."
- Repeat seven times. Keep a natural and comfortable flow throughout, resting in the white light.
- Allow yourself to just "be" in the beautiful, white light.
- There will be no mantra today. Just embrace the feeling.
- Enjoy the Divine Light flowing through your being.
- After a few moments, or when you "feel" you are aware of your present surroundings, breathe the white light into every pore of your being.
- Let it grow into a flame in your heart and just be aware of how you feel.

Journal

Begin your journaling now, remembering to free yourself from expectations. Just be aware of how you feel, and record anything that comes to your conscious mind.

Day Five

Today, you will move through the chakras more quickly. Think of it like moving up a ladder. You will begin the same way that you have.

- As you inhale, relax and take your time. As you exhale the first breath, chant "Lammmmm."
- Relax as you inhale. Repeat as you exhale, "Vammmmm."
- Relax as you inhale. Repeat as you exhale: "Yammmmm."
- Relax as you inhale. Repeat as you exhale: "Hammmmm."
- Relax as you inhale. Repeat as you exhale: "Aaa… oooo… mmmmm…"
- Relax as you inhale. Be in silence for a few moments, or at least seven breaths.
- Be aware of how you feel… Just "be."
- Repeat four times from beginning.

Journal

Conclusion

This week was about connecting to the frequency of each chakra with color and sound. The chant allowed you to use your own voice to align the frequency to its highest place. It is a powerful exercise to do if you need more communication with another, public speaking or just want to relax.

Focus on the color allowed you to exercise your Divine Eye (third eye). As well as practice your visualization. Some never achieve the ability to "see" colors, images and symbols. You should never feel discouraged. Embrace your strengths that you are aware of. Some times you're a feeler or just "know". This is just as powerful as seeing. If you practice Lesson 3 often, you will sensitize the chakra and visualization could become a stronger sense for you. No matter what the outcome please believe you have balanced, harmonized and brought healing to the energy system. The emotions and thought patterns of the subconscious and conscious mind are in harmony.

This will free you to express and manifest from your highest place. There is an unexplainable strength that comes with this and once you are One with this sacred gift you will never let it go.

Below is a chart that shows the chakra, color, sound, and connection to your physical expression. It can also be a simple guide to understanding emotions in each chakra or as a chanting tool for the centers. The Internet is a great place to learn more in-depth on the chakras. "Anatomy of Spirit" by Carolyn Myss is also a great source of information on the chakras.

* Lam
Root Chakra – RED – Security issues; family, tribal, or group power; survival in the physical world

* Vam
Sacral Chakra – ORANGE – Emotional issues; relationship with self and others; finances; inner child; addictive behavior

* Ram
Solar plexus – YELLOW – Self-empowerment and achievement; intuitive center; mental vibration; action in one's life, achievement, and expectations of self

* Yam

<u>Heart Chakra</u> – GREEN – Ability to love self and others; ability to heal lower emotions and thought patterns

* Ham

<u>Throat Chakra</u> – INDIGO BLUE – Faith; communication; free will; expression of creativity; expression of spiritual gifts and abilities

* Om

<u>Brow Chakra</u> – PURPLE – Third Eye; intuitive abilities, clairvoyance; imagination; multi-dimensional view

* Silence

<u>Crown</u> – WHITE – Oneness; compassion; harmony; seeing Self in others;

LESSON FOUR

In lesson four, we will connect to our primal roots. You will take a journey with your Spiritual Guides, Doctors, and Elders. You will be giving the Self and Spirit the gift and power to accept love completely and unconditionally. You will feel and know Oneness with the love and guidance of your Spiritual guides and teachers.

In the physical expression of life, we master the art of giving to others, to the point of neglecting giving the Self and Spirit time to know one another. We give our time; we give what is expected socially, professionally even in matters of the heart. When we give more to another's needs co-dependency can often be a result. In return you can feel unappreciated and neglected even unloved by those around us. It can cause one to go into a helpless state of being and even depression.

When you feel someone drains you or is negative or when you blame others for your own misfortune or unhappiness it is telling you to pay attention to your own Spiritual needs. I prefer the word obligations. We are obligated to nurture our Spirit, still our minds and love the Self. We must learn how and often this is a result of fear. If there is no outlet, (meditation, prayer, creative time are outlets) to receive from our true Divine Source, we will begin to resent others, jobs, finances and put the blame outside of ourselves. We will lash out at those close to us as well as at our Self and even God. Who else, but those closest to us will be affected? This understanding may give you more insight into a relationship from the past as well as the present. Remember energy connections have no time limitation, it is in constant motion.

In the commitment to A Journey to the Light Within,, you have chosen an outlet. Meditation is like recharging a battery; it is a spiritual time-out, a gesture of love to the Self. Spirit and Self rejoice at any moment they become One. They recognize each other, but it is up to you to introduce and nurture this relationship. You are doing just that at this moment.

The breath is always a beginning, as you have seen in previous weeks. Recharging can be achieved in many different ways and expressions. It is the time you take out of the day to just "be" — to stop, to breathe, and to take in nature. To pray, to play, and to laugh. Creative time is also a very powerful outlet — art, music, and dancing, anything that removes you mentally and emotionally from the stressors of life. Yoga is another wonderful way to bring together the body, the mind, and the Spirit.

Stressors appear in everyday life as well as completely unexpected events. We must have a strong mental, emotional and Spiritual relationship with God in order to move through these experiences. It is in the everyday perception and our intention on how to live life we create this foundation. We all experience stress, but what is important is how we respond to it. It is essential to have a strong foundation spiritually, so when unexpected events transpire, we are prepared to handle the consequences. We must nurture our Spirit daily in order to know and to understand who we are, and also to feel a sense of security that no person, no career, and no amount of money can give us. In embarking on this journey, you have chosen to do so and, most importantly, are acting on it. Give your Self a hug!

In this week's lesson, we will give to ourselves love, healing, and light with help from Spiritual Guides, Doctors, and Elders. We all have connection to them. Often, they wait lifetimes to meet us.

Enter into this week's meditation without expectation that you must <u>see</u> them. Allow for the energy to flow, stay with your breathing, and please keep in mind they are with you. This week is a test of faith. Remember: you cannot fool energy. They are not up there deciding that if you do "good" or "right," you will get to meet them. They are with you and have been since your journey on earth began.

The vibration you are opening yourself up to is at a high frequency and, often, emotions can rise. You may feel joy, sadness and at times anxiety. Embrace them all. It is energy moving through you. You are not alone. Breathe through what ever it is.

The more you trust in the process, relax, and focus on whether or not you feel they are here, the more the channels for communication will open for you. You may experience their presence by feeling, inner vision, or a knowing. You may even sense loved ones who have crossed. It is where they all come together to be with you. They come with the highest of intention: to help you.

So let us go now and journey with our Divine Ancestors.

Lesson Four Meditation Assignment

Please read through the assignment once before beginning.

Keep in mind to ask questions, if you have an experience you do not understand while in meditation. For example, if you sense a presence ask, Who are you? Or if you recognize them, embrace them with a hello.

Other possible questions include, What does this mean for me? Keep open to the simplicity of the presence of Spirit Guides, loved ones crossed, etc. They are always with us and often their presence is subtle.

After your meditation, the first line of your entry will be: At this time I feel... Then, write any emotion you're feeling at that moment: sadness, happiness, anxiety, peace, etc. Continue writing any thoughts, feelings, knowings, etc. that come to the conscious mind. Do not try to remember. We are practicing releasing the mental and from self-judgment.

If you do not remember anything, go back to step one. Write your emotions, and go from there. There are no wrong experiences! All will have meaning in the interpretation. This will be the beginning of all meditations. Exceptions are when your experience at the end is just flowing and you need to just let it be written. Share your emotions at this time as well.

A Journey to the Light Within

Prepare for Meditation

Create a comfortable environment. If you are tired, please sit up with your spine straight to keep yourself from falling asleep.

First, create in your mind a sacred shelf or box where you will place all distractions. If your distraction is a person in your life, then you will simply say or think, I place you in the box/shelf at this time to be blessed and in divine order. You may have to do this many times. Or you may not need to do it at all. What is important is that you are letting go of any less-than- positive emotions and/or distractions that would have connected to you and caused even longer and more intense distraction.

Just a reminder again, these sacred tools can be used throughout the week, course, and life!

- Begin with your breath awareness.
- Inhale slowly and comfortably.
- Count silently to four as you take a breath in.
- Exhale to six slowly, comfortably.
- Imagine filling your lower belly with air like a balloon.
- Let the air release naturally; then, gently contract your belly to push out air from your lungs.
- Remember to be as natural as possible. The rhythm will begin to take over after a few moments. TRUST.
- Continue for eight breaths.
- Then increase, inhaling to six and exhaling to eight.
- Allow for eight breaths.
- Allow your breath to flow into a natural rhythm. It will be automatic.
- Tell yourself (silently or aloud) to relax around the eyes, then allow the feeling of calm to drift down to your shoulders, your arms, your hands, your palms, and your fingers.
- Bring your awareness back to your heart, and allow the intention, relaxation, to flow gently down through your torso, your feet, your toes, your breath. Take three breaths.

- Now, bring awareness to your heart light by imagining, seeing, feeling, or knowing that a gold flame is in your heart. Trust… Breathe the light gently with intention and imagination up to the center of your forehead or Divine Eye.

- Hold the light behind the Divine Eye, let it flow back and relax this area for four breaths.

- Simply read along and allow the journey to unfold. This is a conscious meditation. If you start to have another experience, please allow and journal the experience.

- Imagine you are standing facing a tunnel behind your eyes.

- Breathe… Give yourself permission to walk or flow through the tunnel.

- Be aware of your emotions as you pass through the tunnel.

- Begin to follow the path up a mountain.

- Be aware of the mountain — the color green, rocks, snow, etc.

- How do you feel as you ascend? (Focus on your emotions. Close your eyes for a moment and just breathe. Continue when you are ready.)

- As the path nears the peak, you "hear" drumming.

- When you arrive at the peak, you see, feel, or know that there is a circle of spiritual friends (Masters, Guides, and Elders) sitting around a fire.

- Next to them is a teepee. You know you are to go into the teepee.

- You sit in the middle of the teepee on a blanket. Bring your awareness into your breath. Allow yourself to relax and just "be."

- Your awareness is now in the inner light in your heart.

- It illuminates with more light than before.

- This light flows through you. Breathe it down to the soles of your feet. Breathe from your heart, around your shoulders, and into your palms.

- Hold a golden globe of light in each palm.

- Now, breathe from your heart up through your crown, and just allow to flow around you, above and below…

- As you inhale, repeat silently or aloud, "To Receive." As you exhale, repeat "Is to heal." Close your eyes and

- Continue for a minimum of 8 breaths or until you feel relaxed.

- Just be… Embrace the presence of the spiritual friends around you. Thank them for being with you. Remember no expectation for answer.

- Just breathe, naturally and comfortably. Use your mantra, "To receive is to heal," if thoughts or distractions continue. Do not forget your sacred box or shelf, if you need it!

- You will feel when it is time to bring your awareness back to you in the teepee, and when the time to sit up gently in the teepee has come. Trust yourself with this, please. One day it may be a few moments, and the next day it may be 20 minutes. There is no time frame expected of you!

- When it is time to come back, a spiritual friend will take your hand and help you up.

- You will be handed a cup of water. Drink.

- A white robe will be given to you, and you will leave the teepee and find a place in the circle around the fire.

- You will gaze into the fire. Breathe… Just "be."

- As you watch the fire, you "see" the flame reach high into the universe.

- As you breathe, you begin to feel lighter and lighter.

- Relax and smile.

- Know that you are releasing all energy, thought patterns, and emotions that no longer serve you from this moment, this life and every lifetime.

- Breathe and smile…

- The fire is now radiating a beautiful blue light.

- As you breathe in, the blue light comes into your heart light.

- You illuminate and become light. Breathe and just hold yourself in the light.

- You will feel a presence. Embrace your shoulders from behind.

- It is time to leave the sacred circle. The drums are still beating.

- You are embraced by others in white robes, smiling.

- At this time, ask them anything that comes to you.

- Thank them for being with you, and for giving you their love, wisdom, and light.

- You will follow your path… Stop and turn when you see your Spiritual Guides, Doctors, and Elders waiting.

- Know that you can return at any time…

- You are back in your tunnel. Breathe and allow your senses to adjust.

Journal

When you complete meditation, write in your journal your feelings and anything about the experience that comes to your conscious mind.

Day Two

Repeat day one meditation.

Journal

When you complete meditation write in your journal your feelings and anything about the experience that comes to your conscious mind.

Day Three

Before you begin, write a question in your journal that you are looking for guidance on. You have sent the intention for the question. Do not focus on outcome or answer at this moment. Repeat meditation.

Journal

Day Four

Before you begin, write the following in your journal:

What message do you have for me in regards to my Souls ascension?

Journal

When you complete meditation write in your journal your feelings and anything about the experience that comes to your conscious mind.

Day Five

Before you begin, write the following in your journal: "Today I come to my Guides, Doctors, and Elders to receive with an open heart, mind, body, and Soul."

Journal

When you are ready simply journal your emotions at this moment, including anything about the experience that comes to your conscious mind.

Remember: do not worry if you do not feel your question is answered, especially if you are writing. Trust that it will be there. That is what I am here for. If we are working together and there is any confusion, please call or email me. Enjoy your journeys...

Conclusion

This week you made a loving and strong commitment to trust and serve your Spiritual guides, teachers and elders. Your connection begins first with intention. Your desire and faith in their presence fuels the connection. It has been felt and they are with you. As in any relationship it is up to you to nurture this relationship. Which is what you have committed to in the Journeys. Look around at nature, the sky, water, birds and trees. Our masters and teachers are amongst us in nature. This is where we will "feel" them speak to us. Our vibration rises to its highest potential when we connect to nature it is telling the Self it understands and honors Oneness in all.

This week you solidified your relationship with the Divine into your soul's tribal energy. Your spirit is your security and no-one, no degree of wealth can give you what you instilled in your tribal spirit today!

We must not separate our Spiritual journey from our physical. It is one. The spirit needs the body and all its experiences to learn, heal and enlighten. One of the most common complaints is one has no time to practice being more spiritual. IT IS RIGHT OUTSIDE YOUR DOOR! It is when you look at your Self in the mirror, drive your car and enter your workplace. It is how you look a child in the eye or smile at a stranger. Every day you wake you have the stage to practice, the school to learn and so importantly the power to teach! You are embracing this perception or you would not be where you are right now, beginning Lesson 5!

LESSON FIVE

In this lesson the focus will be on the energies of the heart (fourth chakra) and the Divine Eye (sixth chakra). We will be doing this, as you have been, with intention and visualization. Remember: even if you do not "see," you will be open to feel and know the energy connection is being made. Between the heart and Divine Eye is the throat chakra. It's no coincidence that we are in week five and the fifth chakra will be a large part of our exercise. Trust will be important this week. Trust that your Self and Spirit are working together, that your heart and your intuition are one. You are communicating with the language of the Soul. Your cells are embracing this connection and your Divine purpose in motion more than ever.

By now, you are familiar with both of the heart and divine eye charkas — maybe even more familiar than you are consciously aware. In trusting in what you receive a more natural connection is made. This means you will no longer have to "look" for signs or feel alone in meditation or in life.

It will be an automatic state of being, whether you are in meditation or driving in your car or wondering if you should be in a relationship with someone, what career choice to make, even why you are where you are, your intention is heard and will be answered. When relationship with Spirit and Self are nurtured every day you are in a constant state of living consciously and no outside forces "need" to be relied on. Another opinion will be respected but not a needy or helpless force running through you to make your decisions for you.

Your Divine power is at your reach in every breath, every thought and desire. You begin to know what serves you and what does not. You trust in your own spiritual power to guide and your interpretation of the soul's language is your first language.

This is living life in a heightened state of awareness, or living a more "conscious" life. Conscious living is a term we hear a lot these days. The term explains itself: consciousness is a present state of being; subconscious is past. If we stay in the hurts and pains of the

A Journey to the Light Within

past, it will become our present. From here, we create our future. It is perception of our life, our response to how others treat us, and how we treat ourselves that creates the frequency around us. This frequency travels into our body, organs, tissue, blood, etc. and will determine a healthy — or an unhealthy — state of living.

The relationship between your thoughts, your emotions, and your body is constantly in motion. It is your responsibility to nurture this relationship. You have, or you would not be reading this right now! You are responding to your ability to your responsibilities. Do you see how that changes the word responsibility? It takes the pressure off or changes the frequency of what that word can feel like.

We learn to do through daily life experiences. Choices and challenges along the way may cause us, at times, to feel pulled or stressed. This is the body's way of telling you to turn inward or tune into your intuition. Again this becomes a natural response and not a separation between the Self and Spirit.

Faith that Self and Spirit are united is almost an impossible bond to break. Their conflicts with each other become less and when it does begin you will recognize before the pull reaches the lowest point. The most common and personal clue that there is a separation is you feel depressed or anxious. Everyone has low times and we must embrace them, learn from them and heal them. Then we will not create future from the vibration which is running through the energy field.

The body is always sending "clues" via the nervous system, which connects to every system in the physical body. You will then respond with emotional expression or lack of expression. This, in turn, is reflected in your relationships with everything — with your Self, with friends, with your career, and with your finances.

The sacred gift we are born with and are here to open is a true, intimate, and nurturing relationship with a Higher Source, Divine Intelligence,

Christ, Buddha, God. There are so many expressions of the Source from which all is created. With this journey, you are beginning to explore this relationship's possibilities, love and power you hold in the hearts light.

During your meditation time, you will experience and heal lower emotions of, fear, anger, sadness, and uncertainty. They are symbolic through shadows or dark tunnels, with currents of energy running through your body; what is moving the energy through them is your perception of life. This is where the healing process transforms, in your perception of life. Learn and heal! In human nature, we tend to call upon God, angels, loved ones crossed, to "HELP!" when we feel powerless. This will create a low frequency to flow through and the energy to store in the fibers and fluids of the body. All energy will need to express itself and is waiting to create dis-cord even dis-ease. It will also be the catalyst in how you respond to the situations in your life.

All relationships, choices and challenges will be how you can see your Self and Spirit working or not working as One. When we embrace the power within and pray for the acceptance of Divine strength, wisdom and truth we empower instead of energize powerlessness. It is human nature to experiences powerlessness, but it is our free will to give it energy or make it a way of coping with our life. When the relationship with our Self and Spirit is nurtured we become active as opposed to reactive to the situations. The faith, love and compassion carries higher frequency which then can lift the body to its most divine and natural healing frequency.

It will be natural, and you will move through life with strength, confidence, and a sense of Spirit that will always be with you.

You will look forward to being in meditation with the Oneness that flows when Self and Spirit unite. You will nurture your relationship with your Spirit Masters, Guides, and Angels. You will strengthen your relationship with those you have lost in a physical sense. You will soon realize that they are not a loss; through the connection you nurture, you will live in the absence of the perception that anyone or anything can be lost. You will then live in the present and create your future from this place. It is an amazing place to be in life and will help you in times of challenge. You will flow in the eternal rhythm of life, creating the life you deserve.

By bridging the Divine Eye and heart chakra in meditation, you will recognize the love and light that comes from within. The higher frequency created from this union will flow into the physical, strengthening immune system, opening intuitive channels and allowing the Self to express love, creativity and even confidence. Creativity and intuition will flow naturally and lovingly to the Self, a gift your Spirit has been waiting to give since the day you were born.

Here is a reminder about how to begin your sacred time for your lesson. Please do this to get started, if you need. You may be able to simply engage some breathing techniques and begin, but listen to what you need.

Lesson Five Meditation Assignment

Have a notebook, journal, or computer ready so you can write immediately after meditation. Keep in mind to ask questions if you have an experience you do not understand while in meditation. For example, if you sense a presence ask, Who are you? Or embrace them with a hello thank you for your Divine presence at this time.

Other possible questions include What does this mean for me? Keep open to the simplicity of the presence of Spirit Guides, loved ones crossed, etc. They are always with us and, in these quiet times, their presence can be subtle or even very emotional for you to sense.

After your meditation, the first line of your entry will be: At this time I feel... Then, write any emotion you're feeling at that moment: sadness, happiness, anxiety, peace, etc. Continue writing any thoughts, feelings, knowings, etc. that come to the conscious mind. Do not try to remember. We are practicing releasing the mental and from self-judgment.

If you do not remember anything, go back to step one. Write your emotions, and go from there. There are no wrong experiences! All will have meaning in the interpretation. This will be the beginning of all meditations. Exceptions are when your experience at the end is just flowing and you need to just let it be written. Share your emotions at this time as well.

Prepare for Meditation

Create a comfortable environment. If you are tired, please sit up with your spine straight to keep yourself from falling asleep.

First, create in your mind a sacred shelf or box, (folder, use your imagination)! This is where you will place all distractions. Your distraction can come in different forms. For example a person, memory or emotion in your life. Then you will simply say or think, I place you in the box/shelf at this time to be blessed and in Divine order. You may have to do this many times. Or you may not need to do it at all.

What is important is that you are letting go of any less-than-positive emotions and/or distractions that would have connected to you and caused even longer and more intense distraction. Once you connect to the emotion of the experience your vibration will lower. Depending on how much energy has been put into it, through thought, resistance in acceptance, healing, fear will determine how much it will affect you.

You are taking an active stand on energy not serving you. You have given your subconscious permission to let go (Lesson 2) so continue to accept the consequences of this. It is called healing! These sacred tools should be used throughout the lessons, your days and life!

Day One

- Begin with your breath awareness.
- Inhale slowly and comfortably, counting silently to 4 as you breathe in.
- Exhale to 6 slowly, comfortably.
- Imagine filling your lower belly with air like a balloon.
- Let the air release naturally, then gently contract your belly to push out air from your lungs.
- Remember to be as natural as possible. The rhythm will begin to take over after a few moments. TRUST.
- Continue for eight breaths.
- Then, increase your inhalation to 6, and exhale for 8.
- Allow for eight breaths.
- Next, allow your breath to flow into a natural rhythm.
- Bring your awareness to your heart.
- Imagine the inner light (golden flame) in your heart.
- <u>See, feel, or know that this is happening.</u>
- Allow the flame's light to reach the Divine Eye.
- Allow the Divine Eye (forehead area) to fill with light.
- Breathe into this light and let it flow behind the eyes creating a tunnel of light.
- Imagine your self standing, facing the path.
- Begin to step forward on a path.
- Your path will lead you to your bench.
- Ahh, you have returned!
- Sit on the bench, and become comfortable.
- Let's move away from time today… There will be no set time to be on the bench. Just "be."
- When you feel it is time, send out a thank you.
- Say, aloud or silently, Divine Master, may your wisdom fill my being. (Repeat 3 times)
- Breathe, and just be silent on the bench for a bit. Release from expectation, you have been heard.
- Rise from your bench, and follow the path back to the beginning.

- Let your light come back to your heart.
- Bring your awareness to your breath and to your body.
- Allow your senses to adjust.

Journal

Journal, and remember your feelings first! How did you feel sitting with the Divine Master? Excited, nervous, abandoned, loved? Embrace any and all emotions. Share them. Most importantly, know you are not alone.

Day Two

- Begin with your breath awareness.
- You will inhale slowly and comfortably.
- Count silently to 4 as you breathe in.
- Exhale to 6 slowly, comfortably.
- Imagine filling your lower belly with air like a balloon.
- Let the air release naturally, then gently contract the belly to push out air from the lungs.
- Remember to be as natural as possible. The rhythm will begin to take over after a few moments. TRUST.
- Continue for eight breaths.
- Then, increase your inhalation to 6 and your exhale breath to 8.
- Allow for 8 breaths.
- Next, allow your breath to flow into a natural rhythm.
- Bring awareness to your heart.
- Imagine the inner light (golden flame) in your heart. See, feel, or know that this is happening.
- Allow the flame's light to reach your Divine Eye.
- Allow the Divine Eye to fill with light.
- Breathe into this light.
- Imagine yourself standing at the path.
- Begin to step forward on a path.
- Your path will lead you to your bench.
- Sit on the bench, allow yourself to be comfortable.
- Say aloud or silently, "Divine Master, I accept your love and wisdom."
- Breathe, and just be silent on the bench for a bit.
- State your intention. Is there a message for me at this time? For I am open to receive…
- Just "be" for a few moments. Breathe and allow…
- Embrace any presence you feel. No expectations! Just be…
- Close your eyes, and just "be" with their presence.

At this time, you will return to sound, raising the frequency even more around you.

- Inhale silently.
- Exhale the sounds "Yaaammm… Haammm…Oooo..mmm…" 4 times.
- Remember, silence is in the inhale and create the sound on the exhale.

Allow for a few moments of silence after the chanting.
(Refer to week 3 if you need.)
When you feel it is time to leave bench say, "Thank you",

- Breathe the light back into your heart and simply return to your path as before.

Let your senses adjust. Breathe up from the soles of your feet.

Journal

Journal, remembering your emotions first. How do you feel right now? Then, relay the experience, whatever comes to the conscious mind.

Day Three

Today, we are going to be freer with the way we move through our meditation. Make a note of the time, but do not be concerned with how long you "should" meditate.

- Begin with your breath awareness.
- Bring yourself to the heart light. The chant will begin in the heart chakra.
- Inhale silence; exhale "Yam." Repeat 4 times.
- Imagine your Inner Light reaching your Divine Eye.
- Go to your bench. When you arrive, go into the Om ("ahhh… oooo… mmm") Allow for 8 Oms; do more if you like, or just be silent.
- Say or think, "Divine Master, come sit with me. I embrace your love and light. How are we One"… Breathe…
- Your intention is place and as you have done in prior lessons, do not sit in expectation.   Just be… Breathe… Allow…
- Come back when your awareness becomes more present. Always say thank you.
- Even if your senses adjust faster than before that is fine. You may be going into higher states more easily and most definitely consciously by now. Your senses may adjust more quickly as well.

Journal

You will write at this time. Begin with How are we One?

Day Four

In your journal, write a question that you wish wisdom and direction on. Be clear.

If you have more than one keep them separate and set that intention in another meditation.

Repeat Day Three's meditation steps.

Journal

Rewrite your question. Express your emotions

Day Five

Day five is upon you! You will experience the power of receiving with no expectation. You have had this prior, but we are going to place the intention clearly with a mantra. You will be going back to day one of this week. The steps are rewritten for you below.

Create a comfortable environment. If you are tired, please sit up with your spine straight to keep yourself from falling asleep.

First, create in your mind a sacred shelf or box where you will place all distractions. If your distraction is a person in your life, then you will simply say or think, I place you in the box/shelf at this time to be blessed and in Divine Order. You may have to do this many times. Or you may not need to do it at all. What is important is that you are letting go of any less-than- positive emotions and/or distractions that would have connected to you and caused even longer and more intense distraction. These sacred tools can be used throughout the journey, day, and life! Yes, you have heard this before!

Begin with breath awareness.

- Inhale slowly and comfortably, counting silently to 4 as you breathe in.
- Exhale to 6 slowly, comfortably.
- Imagine filling your lower belly with air like a balloon.
- Let the air release naturally, then gently contract the belly to push out air from the lungs.
- Remember to be as natural as possible. The rhythm will begin to take over after a few moments. TRUST.
- Continue for eight breaths.
- Then increase your inhale to 6, and your exhale breath to 8.
- Allow for eight breaths.
- Allow your breath to flow into a natural rhythm.
- Bring awareness to the heart.
- Imagine your inner light (golden flame) in your heart. See, feel, or know this is happening.
- Allow the flame's light to reach the Divine Eye.
- Allow the Divine Eye (forehead) to fill with light.

- Breathe into this light.
- Imagine yourself standing toward a path.
- Being to step forward on a path.
- Your path will lead you to your bench.
- Sit on your bench, become comfortable.
- Say aloud or silently, "Divine Master thank-you for your love, light and wisdom. I accept the divinity in every cell, fiber and fluid of my being."
- Breathe in, and just be silent on the bench for a bit.
- Repeat silently or aloud: on the inhale, "To receive;" on the exhale, "Is to heal."
- Keep your focus on the breath and on the mantra.
- Again, you are moving away from time today. There will be no set time on the bench. Just "be," repeating the mantra.
- When you feel it is time, send out a thank you.
- Rise up from your bench, and follow your path back to the beginning.
- Let your light return to your heart.
- Bring your awareness to your breath and to your body.
- Allow your senses to adjust.

Journal

Conclusion

During this lesson you recognized and nurtured the relationship with your Divine Master. Everyone's belief of Master can be their own. It wo3uld not be fair to say my belief in Christ as Master has to be yours. The Buddha, Divine Mother, Universal Consciousness as well as personal Spirit Guide experiences and angels can be your master.

When we accept and allow this relationship to be our foundation we do fear others beliefs as a threat to our own. Love between Self and Master is a relationship no other can give you or take away once you embrace the Oneness.

It is an eternal union, unique for every individual as well as how they honor it. Your Spirit welcomes this union and the power of the trinity.

Embrace the many emotions that can surface as you sit on your bench. Personally I have cried many tears on my bench as well as held the hand of my Master and knew the power of Divine Love.

Also do not judge if your visits "seem" uneventful. You are keeping the energy doorway open for your Master to communicate. Nothing more is asked of you. Enjoy this relationship and most importantly nurture it by calling upon it.

LESSON SIX

The final lesson of the journey is upon you. You will begin this week's meditation as always, establishing a comfortable environment to meditate. You will begin breath awareness as you have in previous meditations.

Faith and trust in the sacred communication of the Soul is meant to be a natural experience. As we ascend in our physical journey we open the lines of communication with the Soul. Your conscious choice to these journeys is one way of doing just that. Trust all that you have experienced is in your consciousness and will flow naturally through you, when called upon or needed. Again faith and trust in your Spirit is a gift you give your Self and every day an opportunity to be in it.

Your connection to higher levels of consciousness is now clear for you to channel the Divine Intelligence and all that it holds. Being One with Source, all that is Divine, the Universe, God is your Divine privilege.

You have worked very hard in your journey to claim your inheritance. You have set the intention to nurture the relationship with your Self and your Spirit. To live consciously and with highest intentions you will be fulfilling this commitment.

You have learned meditation can be a conscious experience. It can be spontaneous, felt and emotional. It can be seen in nature, a walk or even in an inspirational writing or movie. It can be seen in a loved ones eyes or a child's laugh. It can be experienced in an act of kindness. But you have also learned it can be in sadness, fear or the unknown. In the embracing of all shadows we have an opportunity to allow in the light.

In a commitment to meditation you offer your Self the opportunity to share light with your shadow. This allows for healing and unconditional love and freedom for the Soul to express. It is then you will love and know compassion from the Soul level. Then it is exchanged in all relationships you exist in.

Always begin with a few slow breaths and intention. Each meditation can be different.

A Journey to the Light Within

Release from expectation, as you have practiced in the previous journeys. This is where your faith in the process is tested, but it is so freeing and fulfilling when you trust in it.

Create a comfortable environment. If you are tired, please sit up with your spine straight to keep yourself from falling asleep.

Create your sacred shelf or box where you will place all distractions. Remember if your distraction is a person in your life, then you will simply say or think, I place you in the box/shelf at this time to be blessed and in Divine Order.

Just a reminder, you are letting go of any less-than-positive emotions and/ or distractions that would have connected to you and caused even longer and more intense distraction. These sacred tools can be used throughout the week, course, and life!

- Begin with your breath awareness.
- Inhale slowly and comfortably, tune into the sound of your breath as you breathe in.
- Breathe deeply and comfortably. This should be very natural by now, but even the most disciplined meditator will benefit from the simplicity.
- Imagine filling your lower belly with air like a balloon.
- Let the air naturally release and then gently contract your belly to push air out from your lungs. Tune into the movement of the body,
- Remember to be as natural as possible. The rhythm will begin to take over after a few moments. TRUST.
- Smile…
- Allow your breath to flow into a natural rhythm and just be. Open eyes when you are ready to continue.
- Bring your awareness into your heart light.
- See, feel, or know that there is a beautiful pink rosebud.
- Tune into the petals, the velvety softness. Breathe…
- Allow them to open slowly, as you breathe.
- Allow the color and the energy to fill your heart as you breathe. Let it fill your being.
- Once they've opened, allow for a few more breaths.
- Inhale "Divine" and exhale "Love".

Smile as you do this, eyes closed.

Move away from counting; let the feeling be with you. You will know when to move to next step. Trust yourself.

- Inhale and bring awareness into your throat chakra.
- Connect to the sapphire-blue rosebud.
- Tune into the petals, the velvety softness. Breathe…
- Allow them to open slowly, as you breathe.
- Allow the color and energy to fill your being as you breathe.
- Once they've opened, allow for a few more breaths.
- Inhale "Divine" and exhale "Will".

Like above, smile as you do this, eyes closed.
Again let the feeling be with you. You will know.

- Inhale and bring awareness to your sixth chakra, the Divine Eye.
- Imagine a purple rosebud.
- Tune into the petals, the velvety softness. Breathe…
- Allow them to open slowly, as you breathe.
- Allow the color to fill your being as you breathe.
- Once they've opened, allow for a few more breaths.
- Inhale "Divine" and exhale "Truth".

Like above, smile as you do this, eyes closed.
Again let the feeling be with you. You will know.

- Inhale and bring awareness to the seventh chakra, the crown.
- Imagine a white rosebud. Tune into the petals, the velvety softness.

Breathe…

- Allow them to open slowly, as you breathe.
- Allow the color and energy to fill your being as you breathe.
- Once they've opened, allow for a few more breaths.
- Inhale "Divine" and exhale "Light".

Like above, smile as you do this, eyes closed. Again let the feeling be with you. You will know.
Hold yourself in the white light. Simply read and allow the light to flow.

- Breathe and allow it to flow down, pass by the eyes, cheeks.

Let it flow onto your shoulders, down arms and into your palms. In your palms hold globes of white light.

- Allow it to flow through your torso, legs through the soles of your feet.

Let it flow out of your pores and create an aura of light around you.

- Let the light expand around you. All is light the energy of this light transforms all physicality into light.
- Float in this space…smile…
- Silently repeat while inhaling …"I" exhale "Am."
- Smile. Close your eyes and keep repeating the mantra…there is no time… only light."
- Repeat the mantra and release from time.

When you feel it is time to return, bring awareness to your breath.

- Come down through the light.
- Breathe it in as though every pore is taking it into you.
- Allow it to fill your heart light, and know you have brought it back to you.
- Allow your senses to adjust.

Journal

Relay your feelings at this time, and what comes to your conscious mind…

Day Two

Just create your sacred space. Try being out in nature today if possible. If you cannot physically be outside, take a moment to create an outdoor scene in which you will meditate in. Allow your inner child to be a part of it. Use your imagination! If you can imagine it is real!

Allow your breath to be natural.
Bring awareness into your heart light.

- See, feel, or know that there is a beautiful pink rosebud.
- Tune into the petals, the color, the fragrance, the velvety softness.

Breathe...

- Allow the petals to open slowly, as you breathe.
- Allow the color and energy to fill your heart as you breathe. Let it fill your being.
- Once the petals have opened, allow for a few more breaths.
- Inhale "Divine" and exhale "Love" for a few breaths. Close your eyes, breathe...
- Your awareness will now go deep into the center of the rose. Breathe; go deeper.
- Imagine you are now standing, facing into the rose, and moving into the center.
- You are moving away from Self.
- Faith will allow you see, feel, or know you are on a path that is leading to an entrance of a cave. Breathe as you get closer. Be aware of the feelings you have as you come close to cave.
- Enter the cave slowly, tune into how you feel, your emotions. Just be aware.
- Be aware of what you see, feel, or know.
- Explore for a few breaths, taking your time as you go through the cave.

Be aware of any colors, texture of cave or knowings that come to conscious mind as you explore.

- Find a place to sit, legs crossed, and palms up.
- You will now begin chanting, silently or aloud.
- Inhale Silence; exhale "Yam..."

- Release from the concept of time; just "be" for now with your chant.
- Connect to the echo of the chant resonating through the cave.

You are One with the vibration of the chant. You are One with the energy of the chant.

- Feel when it is done, and sit in silence for a few moments.
  Take a few moments to close your eyes…
  You are transforming lower vibration to higher.
- You are healing all matters of the heart, letting go.
- As you open your eyes a path of rose petals are leading you out of the cave. Pick them up as you go.
- Be aware of how you feel as you exit the cave.
- Smile, and know you can return at any time to heal. Your cave is a sacred site, a quiet place for you to go to. As you leave, there is a white robe outside the cave.
- Release yourself of what you have on, and wrap yourself in the robe.
- Continue to follow the path.
- You come to a waterfall; sit down at the edge of the water, and place the rose petals in the water.
- The waterfall is breathtaking; the mist from the water touches you….
- Watch the petals drift away from the shore, and from you.
- Breathe… Allow… Smile…
- A hand is placed gently on your shoulder.
- The feeling that you are never alone is with you.
- Take a few breaths, release from time, smile…Hold the feeling you are having. You are One with the water, your breath and the peace it offers.
- When you feel it is time allow your senses to adjust. Breathe…
- Open your eyes when ready.

Journal

Remember begin with your feelings.

Day Three

Please read this lesson through once before begin. It is brief, but powerful.

After you read begin your breath awareness. Natural and deep breaths.
You are a master now!

- Bring your awareness to the water, where you left off yesterday; you have never left.
- The hand is still on your shoulder.
- Ask your Spiritual Master (Faith in the presence) to sit with you.

This is any spiritual figure you pray to or are comfortable with — Christ, the Divine Mother, Buddha, Divine Intelligence. The presence may be a knowing.

- Trust that you are not alone.
- Thank them for being with you, and share, "I am with open heart and mind, I am grateful for your presence and guidance on my journey".
- Breathe, and allow the intention to be. <u>Your intention is gratitude.</u>
- Allow the intention to be one with you and your Spiritual Master.
- Thank your Spiritual Teacher for their presence, and express your trust and your feeling of connection. Allow this communication to be natural and in your own words.

Take your time…there is no time…

Tell your Spiritual Master that you look forward to meeting tomorrow.

- Take a deep breath, allowing your senses to adjust. Take a few strong breaths. Smile…

Journal

Remember begin with your feelings.

Day Four

Before you begin today write a question or thought for higher guidance and or healing. Remember intention will be in place. Trust with no expectations. The guidance and healing is here.

- Begin your breath awareness. Allow a sense of peace to flow through you. You have experienced this in previous journeys. It will be more natural and spontaneous.
- Allow your breath to be natural.
- Bring yourself to the waterfall.
- Your Spiritual Master is waiting for you at the water's edge. You look up at the waterfall.
- Sit by your Spiritual Master, and state that you are open to the guidance and healing for the intention you came with.
- Breathe, and just allow silence for a moment.
- Gently lower yourself into the water. Submerge yourself completely, and just "be;" you are comfortable and free.
- Swim slowly or float to the waterfall.
- Allow the healing waters to flow over and around you.
- Tune into the flow of water and energy around and through you.
- Inhale "To receive;" exhale "Is to heal."
- Repeat for a few moments. You will know when you've completed the mantra.
- Release from concept of time. Just be silent. Breathe. Smile…
- Swim under the water toward the shore. As you come up the energy of the night sky, full moon and thousands of stars shining are upon you.
- Lay back on the shore, and look up at the night sky.
- Notice the moonlight glow all around you. Completely relax, melt into the earth below you.
- Breathe…just be for a moment. Close your eyes. No time, you will know when it is time to open your eyes.
- Smile, and send a thank you.
- Your healing. is complete.
- Allow your senses to adjust. Take a deep breath. Smile, send gratitude… There is no time…

Journal

Remember begin with your feelings.

Day Five

Read slowly and begin your breath awareness.

Bring yourself back to the star-lit sky and waterfall. Lying down, gazing at stars. Right where you left off.

- Sit up slowly and be aware of the white roses floating to the water's edge. Reach down, and hold a flower gently in the palms of your hands.
- Allow the fragrance to flow through you. breathe… touch the petals and connect to the velvety softness… Embrace the energy of the rose, breathe…
- A white light illuminates from the flower. <u>Slowly</u> guide the light, close eyes if you like. It flows into your palms, through your arms, and up into your heart. Breathe it down through your torso, legs and through the soles of your feet.
- Breathe it up through your crown, and allow it to flow around you.

Breathe…

- Inhale "I" and exhale "Am;" for as many breaths as you like.
- Allow for silence.
- You understand that the time has come to walk the path again.
- You see a basket and place the roses into it. Carry them back along the path.
- You pass your cave. How do you feel?
- Place the white roses down, in front of your cave. A gentle breeze passes through you.
- Smile and a thank you.
- Continue to follow the path and find a place to rest.

The light is all around you, above, below and around you. You are light; you are free.
Breathe…
Embrace the magic of this moment, the light, the peace, the love, smile…

- Allow awareness to be in the breath and the light that surround you.
- Breathe light up and <u>into</u> the base of your spine.
- With strong breaths, breathe light <u>up</u> your spine.

A Journey to the Light Within

- As light ascends up the spine keep breathing and see, feel or simply trust it is happening for you, with you, because of you.

Let the light exit through the center of your crown, passing through the trees, the clouds, the stars, and the veils of time and space. Breathe…

- Just "be," floating in the light. Breathe here for a few moments. When you feel continue.
- You will become aware of your Spiritual Guide standing between two pillars.
- You bow your head; your Spiritual Master bows their head.
- Thank you flows from your Spiritual Guide's heart to yours.
- You return the feeling in thought or aloud.
- Just "be" for a moment. You will know when to continue.
- Allow your awareness to be in your breath.
- The light in your heart is forever nurtured.
- When you "feel" bring your awareness to the light around you.
- Breathe into your pores. Every pore accepts this light — every cell, all systems, every organ, all fibers and fluids in your physical being accept the light.
- Breathe it deeply back into the heart.

Be aware of your feelings right at this moment. Just be in the silence and energy of giving to you this unconditional love and light.

Take time to breathe and let your senses adjust back to where your journey began. Be aware of the room around you, the sound of your breath as you breathe deeply in.

Take your time grounding. Move fingers, toes and shoulders. Smile. Deep breath.

Stay in silence for a moment and just where you began….breathe…

slowly….smile…

> You are of the light. You are Divine. You are One.
> You carry the Light to share in the sacred silence of your journey.
> In your smile, in your tears, in your joy and in your fears, the Light will shine.
> The facets shine in the midst of all, always to protect you from fall,

The journey of Light is your Divine right, to hold in your heart till physical no more,

Where you then unite with the Masters, who love and guide from the holiest Light

<u>Journal your feelings at this moment…breathe…</u>

CONCLUSION

As one journey ends, another will begin….

In this ending you are now ready for new beginnings.

You have experienced shifts on many levels in your meditations.

You have unleashed subconscious emotional responses, embraced the power of thought and felt the way your body responds to it. So importantly you have nurtured, healed and experienced the natural relationship between Self and Spirit.

There have been tears, fear and euphoria. All natural emotions

You will recognize the signs when separation starts to happen. It becomes more natural to be in a higher state of awareness. You transformed lower frequencies that had settled in your body into a higher frequency. They no longer have "control" over you.

The law of attraction is now in higher frequency and the magnetic attraction that you will create from. It is also your responsibility to keep the vibration. Remember it is your Divine power and you hold the key to freeing it every day. You will attract relationships that free you to express your Divinity, live in your truth and create happiness.

Each meditation led you into higher awareness of the Self, creating a stronger relationship with Spirit. A sacred space to shine light onto your shadows, recognize patterns of fear and helplessness and transform them into divine opportunities to learn and heal.

You are free to experience a happy and healthy relationship with Self and create the life you so deserve. Inner strength will feel more natural and in this transformation guide you through the choices and challenges in the journey ahead.

We would be unrealistic to think there are no challenges on the path ahead. But you now know how call upon the inner strength within.

You will in turn honor your Soul and express your Divinity and its journey in the world of physical expression.

The Self and Spirit can work together in facing the shadows of our personality. As you know now, this is where we store the energy from experiences of confusion, fear, sadness, and anger. All of these emotions are energy carrying a low frequency. Or as we more humanly put it, negative or bad.

There will be physical manifestation of all energy, it will express itself and is fueled by emotions connected to the experiences. This energy can be in the subconscious and conscious mind. As you learned when unexpected knowings appeared, whether in form of person or experiences. It is the subconscious this energy will remain unless we heal the unresolved emotions and pattern of thought.

In the Let Go / Let In you learned the power of separating the two. Being aware of the lower thought pattern energies you attain the power to learn, heal and adjust them. But they first must be recognized, embraced and felt. Then you are free to set free. In the understanding of how you function as an energy, you understand the language of the Soul.

The journey has revealed to you many responses — some, you have enjoyed; others may have made you feel (really, released) anxiety, anger, and sadness. This is the body's way of saying, Let me out. Whether it was expressed in a dream, during a meditation, or just going through the day, it wanted to be released. You hold the key to the release, in intention you give permission for this release.

Now you no longer hold this energy and the magnetics will no longer pull to you lessons to be learned form it. It is empowering and life-shifting. It is forever with you as are the tools to keep energy moving. You will live in your present more aware and create your future from this vibration now.

The questions "why am I here" or "what is my purpose" are answered in personal transformation and healing. To know the spirit is to know and guide the Self to the higher truth and awareness. The truth of the life lies within ones heart and mind. Recognizing and embracing this sacred power is an important part of our journey. Our relationship with the Divine, embracing eternal life and healing are the opportunities we have to release this power, humbly and with compassionately.

There is a responsibility to this transformation and as you have experienced, you are responding to your abilities as a Spiritual being in the physical expression of the Soul.

To transcend fear into strength, anger into compassion and all into love. Your future now is manifesting from a higher frequency or in other words a Divine expression. This is because of your conscious choice to get to know who you really are.

To embrace this truth is to free the soul to Its journey into light. To know you hold the sacred power to shine light into the dark.

Thank you for letting me share the journey with you. Peace and love.

Beth Lynch

For information on taking me on the Journeys with you, Services, Events, or to speak on Meditation, Healing, Channeling and the Spiritual-Science of living in the world today email info@innerlightteaching.com or visit www.innerlightteaching.com

Phone: 888.271.4487

Printed in the United States
By Bookmasters